CAMBRIDGE PRIMARY
English

Activity Book

3

Gill Budgell and Kate Ruttle

CAMBRIDGE
UNIVERSITY PRESS

University Printing House, Cambridge CB2 8BS, United Kingdom

Cambridge University Press is part of the University of Cambridge.

It furthers the University's mission by disseminating knowledge in the pursuit of education, learning and research at the highest international levels of excellence.

Information on this title: education.cambridge.org

First published 2015
7th printing 2016

Printed in Dubai by Oriental Press

A catalogue record for this publication is available from the British Library

ISBN 978-1-107-68235-1 Paperback

Contents

1 Setting the scene

 A Look at these words. Underline the nouns and ring the adjectives.

mountain	butterfly	book
interesting	beautiful	office
rabbit	young	happy
clever	shirt	rain
sharp	blue	

B Take a photo of the view from a window and stick it in the box, or draw a picture of what you can see from the window. Label at least six different things in the picture, using an adjective and a noun in each label, such as *blue sky, white clouds*.

> Nouns are names of people or things – such as *cat, book*. Adjectives describe nouns – a *pretty* cat, a *long* book.

2 An ordinary school day

 A What would make an ordinary school day extraordinary for you? Would it be:

- winning or achieving something?
- a sudden event?
- an unexpected visitor?
- an exciting lesson?
- or even an exciting fantasy event?

1 Draw a picture of an extraordinary school day.

2 Label six things that make it extraordinary.

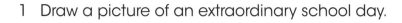

B Re-read the opening sentence of *Once upon an Ordinary School Day* by Colin McNaughton.

Once upon an ordinary school day, an ordinary boy woke from his ordinary dreams, got out of his ordinary bed, had an ordinary wash, put on his ordinary clothes and ate his ordinary breakfast.

1 List all the adjectives.

ordinary _____

_____

2 List all the nouns.

_____

_____

3 The power of words

 A Complete the letters of the alphabet in English.

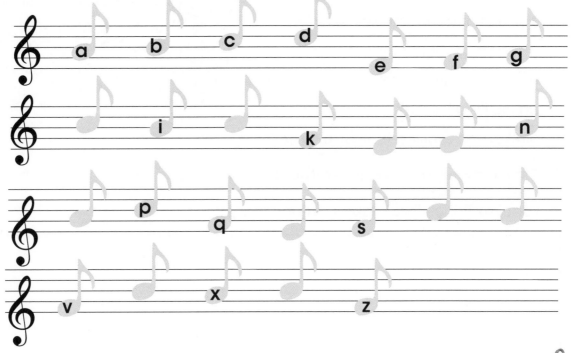

B Write these words in alphabetical order in the table. Then find the words in a dictionary and write what they mean.

> thunderous   crash   ordinary   wonderful   extraordinary

Words are listed in alphabetical order in dictionaries..

Word	Meaning

A Which words would you use to describe the pictures?

1 Complete the description of picture A.

It is a _____ day. The sky is _____

so everyone feels _____ . Some people

are arriving. They are feeling _____ as

they walk towards the mall. Others have

spent a _____ time in the shops. They

look _____ as they walk back to their cars.

A

2 Now complete the description of picture B.

It is a _____ day. There is a _____

storm. The sky is _____ so everyone

feels _____ . The people who are arriving

are feeling _____ as they walk towards

the mall. Other people are leaving. They

look _____ as they hurry back to their cars.

B

 **B** Read this description.

It was a ¹ **nice** day so we decided to go to the beach. I was feeling ² **happy**.
The beach was ³ **nice** and all the people were ⁴ **happy**. I wanted to paddle
in the sea. The water felt ⁵ **nice**. After my paddle, I had a ⁶ **nice** ice cream.
"I am ⁷ **happy**," I told my mum. "Thank you for such a ⁸ **nice** day out."

Improve the description by choosing a more descriptive word to replace the
eight words in bold. Try to use different words each time. Write your words here.

1 _____   2 _____

3 _____   4 _____

5 _____   6 _____

7 _____   8 _____

5 Characters

 A On page 13 of the Learner's Book you read a character portrait of Liang. Now create a different character for Liang. This time he could

- love music

- be interested in fashion

- love sport.

Write your character portrait here.

_____

_____

_____

_____

_____

B Match the adjectives on the left with the adjectives on the right that mean nearly the same thing.

friendly	enthusiastic
happy	occupied
kind	delighted
busy	welcoming
interested	considerate
excited	engrossed

You may need to use a dictionary or a thesaurus.

6 Verbs

 Look at the sentences. Are they in the past, present or future tense? Underline the verb in the sentences. Then write past, present or future for each sentence.

Example: He _had_ a cup of chai after school. _____past_____

1   The phone rings all day long. _____

2   Daddy will be home after your bedtime. _____

3   We are all here today. _____

4   The baby owls learnt to fly. _____

5   The cake will be cooked in five minutes. _____

6   Hidaya picked her friends for her cricket team. _____

7   The tree outside my window grows very fast. _____

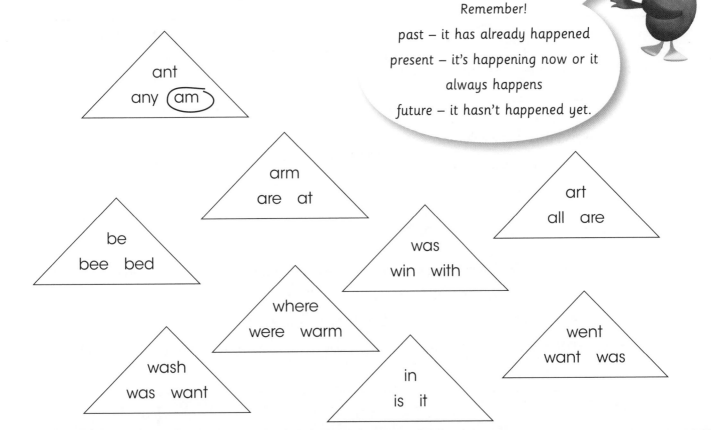

Look at these groups of words. Circle the forms of the verb *be* in each triangle.

Remember!

past – it has already happened

present – it's happening now or it always happens

future – it hasn't happened yet.

ant
any (am)

arm
are   at

art
all   are

be
bee   bed

was
win   with

where
were   warm

wash
was   want

in
is   it

went
want   was

A Make word webs to show the meanings of these words. Use a thesaurus to help you.

means the same =
thrilling

means the same =

sounds a bit the same =

means the same =

means the opposite =

EXCITING

looks a bit the same =

means the opposite =

means the opposite =

means the same =

means the same =

sounds a bit the same =

means the same =

means the opposite =

whispered

looks a bit the same =

means the opposite =

means the opposite =

B Finish the story that Grace was thinking about.

We were lost. Our ship was sinking and we were miles away from anywhere. Everyone was giving up hope. But I felt brave. So I climbed to the very top of the mast and I looked around me as hard as I could. The minutes went by slowly. Then, suddenly, I saw something.

"Look!" I cried. _____

_____

_____

_____

_____

_____

_____

_____

_____

_____

_____

_____

_____

8 Dialogue

 A Read this short dialogue

1 Using a blue pencil, underline the words that Mihu said.

2 Using a green pencil, underline the words that her son Yuu said.

"Where are you going?" shrieked Miho, as Yuu ran off.

Yuu looked over his shoulder and shouted, "I'll be back later, mother."

Much later, when Yuu came home, his mother was waiting for him. "Where have you been?" she demanded. "I have been so worried!"

"I'm sorry," mumbled Yuu. "I had forgotten to do something important, but then I remembered it."

"Nothing is that important," complained Miho. "Boys should do what their mother tells them to do."

"But this was very important!" declared Yuu. "I had forgotten to get your present. But then I remembered. Look!" He held out a small box.

"You are a good boy!" stated Mihu, giving Yuu a kiss and rubbing his head.

B List all the verbs in the dialogue that could be replaced by *said*.

<u>shrieked</u>

_____

C Rewrite the verbs from Activity B in alphabetical order.

_____

_____

9 Sequencing events

 A Choose a story you know. Decide on the six main ideas or events in the story and write them on the story mountain.

Title: _____

Author: _____

3 Development	4 Exciting part

2 Beginning/Problem	5 Then what happens?

1 Introduction	6 Ending

B Answer these questions about your chosen story.

1 Who is the main character in the story?

_____

2 Write three adjectives to describe the main character.

_____ _____ _____

3 Who are the other important characters?

_____

_____

4 Where is the story set?

_____

5 Write three adjectives to describe the setting.

_____ _____ _____

10 Plan a story

A It's easy to forget to use capital letters and full stops when you're writing a story. The writer of this story has forgotten some of them. Make the following corrections to the story.

1 Change four letters to capital letters.

2 Add the five missing full stops.

Marco loved riding his bike but he was getting too big for it he needed a new bike but he knew his papa didn't have enough money one day he saw a notice for a bike race the prize was a new bike marco wanted that new bike but first he would have to win the race on his little bike

B It's also easy to forget the correct spelling of words. Complete the following spelling log. You can use a spelling log like this one for other words that are difficult to spell too. Add two new words that you find tricky to remember.

Word	Tricky bit	Word	Similar word	Similar word
was	wa	was	want	what
said	ai	said	again	
other	o	other		

11 Write a story

Grace was a girl who loved stories.

She didn't mind if they were read to
her or told to her or made up out of her
own head. She didn't care if they were from
books or on TV or in films or
on the video or out of Nana's long memory.
Grace just loved stories.

And after she had heard them, or sometimes
while they were still going on, Grace would
act them out. And she always gave herself the most exciting part.

One day at school her teacher said they were going to do the play of *Peter
Pan*. Grace put up her hand to be … Peter Pan.

"You can't be called Peter," said Raj. "That's a boy's name."

But Grace kept her hand up.

"You can't be Peter Pan," whispered Natalie. "He wasn't black."
But Grace kept her hand up.

"All right," said the teacher. "Lots of you want to be Peter Pan, so
we'll have to have auditions. We'll choose the parts next Monday."

When Grace got home, she seemed rather sad.

"What's the matter?" asked Ma.

"Raj said I couldn't be Peter Pan because I'm a girl."

"That just shows all Raj knows about it," said Ma. "Peter Pan is *always* a girl!"
Grace cheered up, then later she remembered something else. "Natalie says
I can't be Peter Pan because I'm black," she said.

Ma started to get angry but Nana stopped her.

"It seems that Natalie is another one who don't know nothing," she said.
"You can be anything you want, Grace, if you put your mind to it."

From *Amazing Grace* by Mary Hoffman

Read the story and answer the questions.

1 What did Grace like doing? Tick (✓) the correct answer.

a She liked writing stories. ☐

b She liked reading stories. ☐

c She liked hearing stories. ☐

2 What did Grace do when the story was finished?

_____

_____

3 Did Grace want to be in the play? How do you know?

_____

_____

4 Why was Raj wrong?

_____

_____

5 Nana thought Grace could be Peter Pan. What did she say to Grace?

_____

_____

6 Tick all the reasons the other children gave for why Grace could not be Peter Pan

her name is Grace ☐

she is too tall ☐

she is a girl

her hair is too long ☐

she is black ☐

12 Improve your story

 A Choose five words from your writing that were difficult to spell. Write them in the first column of the spelling log and complete the log.

Word	Tricky bit	Word	Similar word	Similar word

2 Let's have a party!

1 Celebrations

A Find these 20 words in the wordsearch. The words can go across or down.

anniversary birthday
carnival ceremony
enjoy ~~family~~ feast
festival fiesta friends
fun games happy
jolly laugh meal
meet parade
party performance

All the words are linked to celebrations!

F	A	M	I	L	Y	E	H	A	P	P	Y
R	B	O	L	I	P	A	R	A	D	E	S
A	N	N	I	V	E	R	S	A	R	Y	M
N	T	H	E	G	R	E	O	N	U	F	E
T	F	F	L	A	F	T	R	N	M	I	A
C	E	R	E	M	O	N	Y	I	S	E	L
P	S	I	T	E	R	A	F	E	A	S	T
A	T	E	E	S	M	E	E	T	I	T	G
R	I	N	F	C	A	R	N	I	V	A	L
T	V	D	U	I	N	K	J	H	U	N	A
Y	A	S	N	N	C	J	O	L	L	Y	U
A	L	W	F	T	E	N	Y	O	D	O	G
B	I	R	T	H	D	A	Y	Z	I	N	H

B Draw a picture, or stick in a photo, of a celebration you enjoyed. Label the five people or things in your picture that were most important to you.

2 A class party

A Look at the recipe for salt dough.
Using a red pencil, circle all the verbs.

How to make salt dough

You will need

2 cups of flour

1 cup of salt

1 cup of warm water

A cup for measuring

A large mixing bowl

A spoon

An airtight container

What to do

1   Mix together the flour and salt in a large bowl.

2   Slowly stir in the warm water.

3   Mix well until the mixture feels like dough.

4   Use your hands to push the mixture into a ball.

5   Kneed for at least five minutes or until smooth.

6   Put the salt dough in an airtight container to keep it soft.

Any volunteers?

B Write three things that tell you that *How to make salt dough* is an instruction text.

1 _____

2 _____

3 _____

Try making some salt dough for yourself. You can store the salt dough in an airtight container for up to a week.

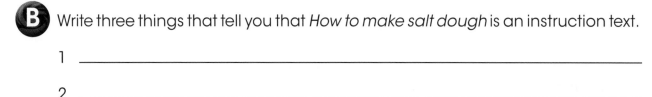

3 Fiction or non-fiction?

 A Read text 1 on page 21 and answer the questions.

1   Is text 1 fiction or non-fiction?

_____

2   Which three features help you to answer question 1?

_____

_____

3   Why has someone written this text?

_____

4   Who would read this text?

_____

5   What type of text is text 1?

_____

B Read text 2 and answer the questions.

1   Is text 2 fiction or non-fiction?

_____

2   Which three features help you to answer question 1?

_____

_____

3   Why has someone written this text?

_____

4   Who would read this text?

_____

5   What type of text is text 2?

_____

How to make a sponge cake

You will need

175 g softened butter, sugar and flour

3 medium eggs

1 tsp baking powder

What to do

1   First mix together the butter and the sugar.
2   Add the eggs and beat until smooth and creamy.
3   Now mix the baking powder in with the flour.
4   Then sift the flour into the butter mix and gently fold in.
5   Finally spoon the mixture into two shallow cake tins and
    bake in a medium oven for 25 minutes.

Amelia   2
is invited to
Vovó's Surprise Party.
It will be at: Santa Teresa Colombo Café
                    Rio de Janeiro
on 18th May at 4.30.
Come dressed to impress.
RSVP

4 Instructions

 A Order the words to give the instructions for making a pop-up card.

1   the / first / in / card / half / fold

_____

2   fold / card / next / small / the

_____

3   stick / big / card / the / small / into / card / the

_____

4   a / draw / picture / then

_____

5   the / on / picture / the / card / stick / small / finally

_____

Remember! Look for command verbs or sequencing words to start each line, and don't forget the capital letters and full stops!

B If you add *tion* to each of these beginnings of words, does it make a real word? Write the word if it is a word. Cross out any word beginnings that don't make a word with *tion*.

instruc ___tion___

1 pic _____

2 sa _____

3 decora _____

4 sta _____

5 ca _____

6 fic _____

7 direc _____

8 dac _____

9 explora _____

10 informa _____

11 atten _____

5 Write an invitation

 A Read the following paragraph. Then use the information to complete the invitation.

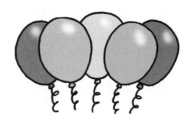

Thursday, 9 November

I saw Lisha today. She said that she was going to invite Mbeke to her birthday party on 18th November. Lisha said that her party will be at the New Club on Ikwere Road. It sounds like it will be a great party because everyone has to go dressed as an animal! Lisha wants everyone to have some of her birthday cake so she's having the party from 3pm until 5pm.

party

Dear _____

You are invited to

_____

It will be at

_____

_____

on _____

at _____

B Underline the verb in these sentences. Then rewrite the sentences in the past tense.

Example: Lisha <u>plans</u> a party.

<u>Lisha planned her party.</u>

1 She invites all her friends.

_____

2 She wants to play lots of games.

_____

3 It is the day of Lisha's party.

_____

4 All her friends are at her house.

_____

5 But Lisha is in bed.

_____

6 Poor Lisha is not well!

_____

6 More instructions

A Decide whether the sentences come from an instruction text. Tick (✓) the ones you think are instructions.

1 First, put the egg in the water. ☐

2 It is not a good idea to push people in the playground. ☐

3 Be kind to each other. ☐

4 When it's dry, turn the paper over. ☐

5 I made a cake yesterday. First, I went and bought some flour. ☐

6 Add the milk and stir. ☐

B What sort of word? Write these words in the correct box.

battery ~~classroom~~ conversation cucumber different disagree fingernail helpful instruction letterbox midnight mountain outside remember teapot understand unhappy upstairs

Compound words	Words with a prefix or suffix	Other long words
classroom		

7 Party food

A Look at these two pages of text and answer the questions.

1 Which is the contents page, text A or text B?

_____

Text A

Healthy drinks

Nutty banana whirl	28
Orange refresher	28
Honey and yoghurt smoothie	29

Ways with fruit

Fruit rockets	31
Orange oat biscuits	32
Carrot slice	33

Text B

Apple 27, 35	Melon 31
Apricots 16, 21, 26	Milk 24, 28
Banana 24, 28, 31	Nuts 17, 28, 35
Butter 13, 32, 33, 34	Oats 16, 26, 32
Carrot 33	Orange 6, 17, 28, 29
Flour 19, 23, 32, 22	Orange juice 28
Honey 15, 21, 28, 29	Pineapple 31
Jelly 17, 26, 35	Strawberry 31, 34
Lemon 16, 23, 25	Sugar 16, 33, 37
Lemon juice 28	Watermelon 31
Lime 5, 28	Yoghurt 28, 29, 34

2 What kind of text is the other text?

_____

3 Would you find text A at the beginning, in the middle or at the end of
a book?

_____

4 Where would you find text B – at the beginning, in the middle or at the end
of a book?

_____

5 Which two healthy drinks would you find on page 28?

_____

6 Which page would you go to if you wanted to make fruit rockets?

_____

7 Which three pages have recipes that use bananas?

_____

8 Which page has a recipe that uses pineapple?

_____

A Put these ingredients in alphabetical order as if they were in an index.

> milk   butter   cheese   yoghurt   flour   sugar
> salt   beans   tomato   bread   toast   biscuits

_____   _____   _____

_____   _____   _____

_____   _____   _____

_____   _____   _____

B Look at these pairs of words. Write a sentence that shows the meaning of each word.

Don't forget the alphabet!

a b c d e f g h i j k l m
n o p q r s t u v w x y z

1 noisy

_____

2 noisily

_____

3 slow

_____

4 slowly

_____

5 happy

_____

6 happily

_____

9 Party games

A Draw a picture of a game you enjoy playing at parties. Label the things you need for the game.

B Write instructions for playing the game.

_____

_____

_____

_____

_____

_____

_____

_____

10 Plan a game

 A Do you know how to spell these common words?

after again ~~any~~ ~~because~~
behind ~~every~~ half have here
~~many~~ ~~most~~ ~~one~~ ~~only~~ some
~~sure~~ their ~~these~~ they

You need good spelling to write instructions.

Use the words in the box words to complete the words below.

1 t_e _

2 _ _ _ e _

3 be ca u s e

4 Su re

5 m o s t

6 o n l y

7 a n y

8 t h e s e

9 a g a i n

10 e v e r y

11 o n e

12 m a n y

13 _ _ l _

14 _ e _ _

15 _ _ e _ _

16 _ _ v _

17 _ e _ i _ _

18 _ _ _ e

B Write three tips for working out how to spell a tricky word.

1 _____

_____

2 _____

_____

3 _____

_____

11 Write instructions

Well, you all need to sit in a circle.

Everyone has to be quiet.

You need to get your paper mouse.

Everyone holds onto the tails.

I got the cone.

I had to bang the cone down on the mice.

Everyone had to try to pull their mice out.

A Pretend you are a teacher. Read the instructions for the game. What has the writer done well? Is there anything that could be improved? Write notes on the instructions to give the writer feedback.

B Rewrite the instructions for the game, correcting any mistakes you found and following the feedback you gave in Activity A.

_____

_____

_____

_____

_____

_____

12 Improve your instructions

 Answer these questions about what you have learnt in Unit 2.

1 What have you learnt about instructions? Write three things.

_____

_____

_____

2 Why were instructions useful when you were planning your party?

_____

_____

3 Which other text types were useful for planning your party? Why?

_____

_____

4 What did you most enjoy doing in this unit?

_____

_____

3 See, hear, feel, enjoy

1 Breakfast

A Write the name of the senses.

_____   _____   _____

_____   _____

B Complete the sentences with the things you enjoy experiencing using your senses.

1 I like to taste _apples because_ _____

_____

2 I like to smell _____

_____

3 I like to see _____

_____

4 I like to hear _____

_____

5 I like to touch _____

_____

Write the words in the correct petals.

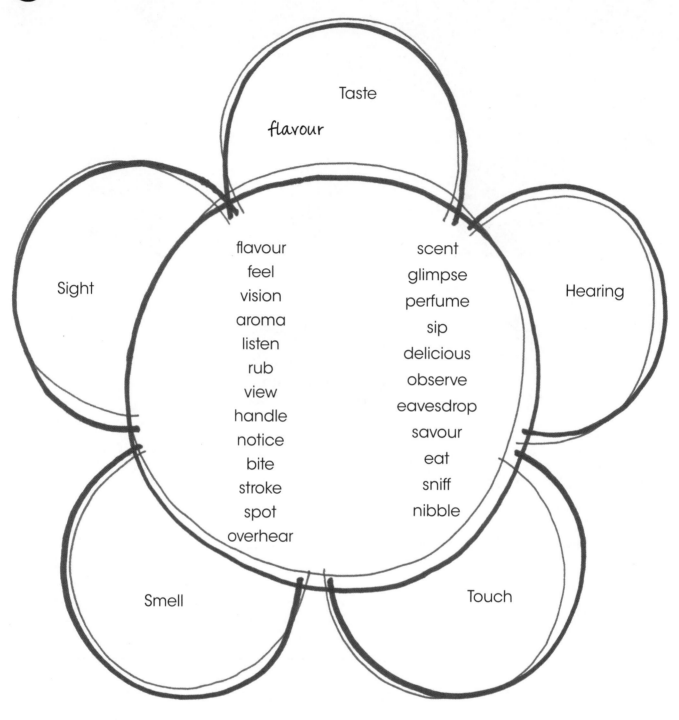

Taste

flavour

Sight

flavour
feel
vision
aroma
listen
rub
view
handle
notice
bite
stroke
spot
overhear

scent
glimpse
perfume
sip
delicious
observe
eavesdrop
savour
eat
sniff
nibble

Hearing

Smell

Touch

1   Which sense has most words?

_____

2   Why do you think some sense have more words than others?

_____

2 Poem to play script

 A Look at these words. Are they nouns or adjectives? Write the words in the correct cloud.

Language focus

The suffix *ly* is often – but not always – used to make an adjective into an adverb, telling you how something is done: *excited* + *ly* → *excitedly*, *thoughtful* + *ly* → *thoughtfully*.

For most words that end in *y*, change the *y* to an *i* before adding *ly*: *happy* + *ly* → *happily*, *busy* + *ly* → *busily*.

For words ending in *le*, take off the *le* before adding *ly*: *comfortable* + *ly* → *comfortably*, *horrible* + *ly* → *horribly*.

firm   → _____   easy   → _____

comfortable → _____   calm   → _____

tired   → _____   double → _____

sleepy   → _____   polite   → _____

bad   → _____   lucky   → _____

B Read this short text. Then answer the questions.

It was Sanjay's birthday. All day long he had looked at his pile of presents. He really wanted a kite, but he couldn't see any present that was kite-shaped.

At last it was time for him to open his presents: video games, socks, colouring pens, a cricket bat. As Sanjay opened each present he felt sadder and sadder.

Finally there was only one present left. It was a long, thin box from his sister Nargis. He looked at her and she smiled back at him. He ripped the paper off the box … Was it …? It was! It was a kite! It was the red kite they had seen in the market the previous week. Sanjay carefully unfolded the kite before he looked up at Nargis and smiled.

1 Why was Sanjay having presents?

_____

2 What time of day was it when Sanjay opened his presents? How do you
know? Write the words that tell you.

_____

3 List three presents that Sanjay opened.

_____ _____ _____

4 Why did Sanjay feel sad when he opened his presents?

_____

5 What did Nargis give Sanjay?

_____

6 Write two things you know about Nargis.

_____

_____

7 Write two things you know about the kite.

_____

_____

3 Write a play script

Later that evening Sanjay was talking to his sister. "How did you know I
wanted that kite?" he asked.

"How did I know?" she repeated. "Every day for the past two weeks you
have made me go with you to the kite stall in the market to look at it."

"Well," said Sanjay, "I really like it. Thank you."

"Good," replied Nargis. "You know that it's my birthday in three weeks,
don't you?"

"Yes," said Sanjay hesitantly.

"Well, I want you to come to the market with me tomorrow. I want to show you something."

"OK," said Sanjay. "You got me the present I wanted, so I'll get you the present you want."

"I knew you'd understand," smiled Nargis.

A Read the dialogue between Sanjay and Nargis, his sister. Then rewrite the dialogue as a play script.

_____

_____

_____

_____

_____

_____

_____

_____

_____

_____

_____

_____

_____

B Write three adjectives to describe Sanjay.

_____ _____ _____

Write three to describe Nargis.

_____ _____ _____

New sights

I like to see a thing I know
Has not been seen before,
That's why I cut my apple through
To look into the core.

It's nice to think, though many an eye
Has seen the ruddy skin,
Mine is the very first to spy
The five brown pips within.

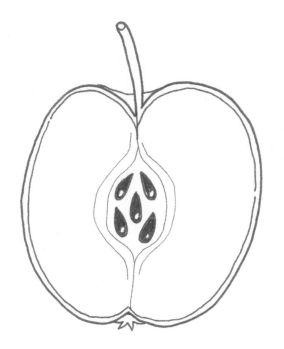

Anonymous

 Read the poem then answer the questions about it.

1   Which fruit is the poem about?

    _____

2   What does the poet want to look at?

    _____

3   Write two sets of words from the poem which rhyme.

    _____ and _____

    _____ and _____

4   What has *many an eye* seen?

    _____

5   What does the poet see that no-one else has ever seen?

    _____

6   What do you think the word *ruddy* means in the line *Has seen the ruddy skin*?

_____

B Find another poem that is about or which mentions food. Copy at least four lines of it here.

_____

_____

_____

_____

_____

_____

_____

_____

_____

5 Write a poem

Frog

Water animal

You swim

in a pond.

You sit still and catch flies

with your tongue.

Frog

Hopping pond-dweller

Swim with webbed feet

across the pond's scummy surface;

Sit statue-still. Snatch a fly

with a quick flick of your sticky-tape tongue.

 Read the two poems called 'Frog'.

Plan a new poem, about a different animal, based on the 'Frog' poems.

Name of animal _____

What does the animal do? List some powerful verbs.

_____   _____

_____   _____

What does the animal look like? List some powerful noun phrases.

_____   _____

Write your poem here.

_____

_____

_____

_____

_____

_____

B Change at least three things to make your poem more descriptive.
Then write your improved poem here.

---

6 Publish your poem

A Think of a cat. Circle the best word each time for a cat.

1 What does it **look** like?   thin   sleek   funny   elegant   neat

2 How does it **feel**?   fluffy   furry   thairy   smooth   rough

3 What **sound** does it make?   loud   purr   howl   meow   silent

4 What does it **do**?   pounce   sit   sleep   stalk   watch

5 How does it **move**?   suddenly   slowly   smoothly   statue-still   quickly

B Change at least three things to make your poem more descriptive.
Then write your improved poem here.

---

4 Fiery beginnings

1 A roaring fire

 A Write each of the fire words in a box below to show which kind of word each one is.

Some of the words will fit into more than one box.

Nouns	Verbs	Adjectives

glowing   blaze   fiery

shining   brilliant   flickering

sparkle   dwindle   flame

B Choose one noun, one verb and one adjective from the fire. Write one sentence containing all three of these words.

_____

_____

Bear and Fire

In the beginning, Bear owned Fire.
Fire warmed Bear and his people on cold days
and it gave them light when the nights were
long and dark. Bear always carried Fire with him.

One day, Bear and his people went to a forest.
Bear put Fire down at
the edge of the forest, then Bear and his people
went deeper and deeper into the forest to look for food.

Fire blazed up happily for a while until it had burned nearly all of its wood.
It started to smoke and flicker, then it dwindled down and down. Fire was
worried. It was nearly out. "Feed me! Feed me!" shouted Fire. But Bear and his
people had wandered deep into the forest, and they did not hear Fire's cries.

At that moment, Man came walking through the forest and saw the small,
flickering Fire. "Feed me! Feed me!" cried Fire.

"What should I feed you?" Man asked. He had never seen Fire before.

"I eat sticks and logs," Fire replied.

Man picked up a stick and gave it to Fire. Fire sent its flames flickering up the
side of the stick until the stick started to burn. Man brought more
and more sticks and Fire leapt and danced in delight.

Man warmed himself by the blazing Fire, enjoying the colours of the flames
and the hissing sound Fire made as it ate the wood. Man and Fire were very
happy together and Man fed Fire sticks whenever it got hungry.

A long time later, Bear and his people came back to the edge of the forest,
looking for Fire. Fire was angry when it saw Bear and it jumped and
roared at him and drove him away.

So from that day to this, Fire has belonged to Man.

A Re-read the myth 'Bear and Fire' then answer the questions.

1 What did Fire give Bear at the beginning of the story? Tick (✓) two things.

people ☐   cold ☐   warmth ☐   light ☐   dark ☐

2 Where did Bear put Fire while he looked for food?

_____

3 Why didn't Bear keep Fire with him in the forest?

_____

4 How did Fire feel when Bear first left him? Tick(✓) one adjective.

happy ☐   sad ☐   frightened ☐   lonely ☐

5 Write one word from the text that tells you how Fire felt. _____

6 Why didn't Bear come to feed Fire?

_____

7 Who fed Fire when Bear didn't come?

_____

8 What did he feed Fire and how did he know what to give Fire to eat?

_____

9 Why did Fire drive Bear away?

_____

10 This story is a myth because

a it doesn't have very many characters. ☐

b it isn't a true story. ☐

c it's an old story from Native Americans. ☐

d it explains why people have fire. ☐

B Ask your family and friends about myths from where you live. Write your favourite myth in your notebook and share it with the class.

3 Pronouns

A Write the words in the correct boxes.

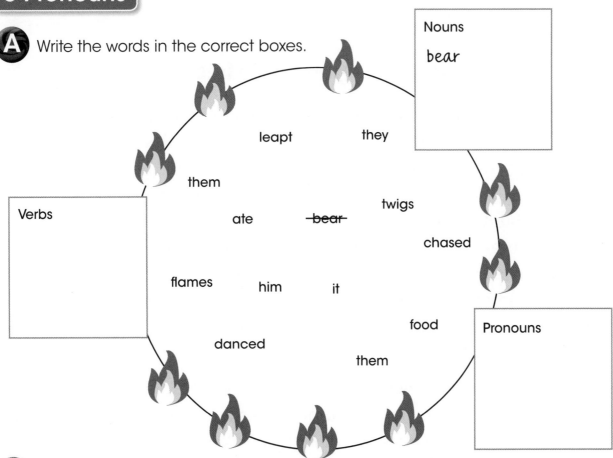

Nouns
bear

Verbs

Pronouns

leapt they

them

ate ~~bear~~

twigs

chased

flames him it

food

danced

them

B Read this paragraph and underline all the pronouns. Then complete the table.

Fire was worried. It had almost gone out. But Man heard its calls for help and he came. Fire told Man what it liked to eat and Man went to look for twigs and sticks. He placed them down beside Fire. While Fire devoured them, Man warmed himself.

Nouns or noun phrase	Pronouns
Fire	
Man	
twigs and sticks	

A Read the story.

King Solomon and the Queen of Sheba

[1] Over 3500 years ago, the Queen of Sheba began to hear strange tales. The traders who came to her African kingdom told tales of a new king. "King Solomon," they said, "is a very wise man." As she sat and bargained with the traders deep into the night, she asked them questions about this new king. She watched their faces in the flickering light of the fires and saw that in the stories they told her about the king, they spoke the truth. "There are already legends about this man," she said to her closest advisers. "I must meet him so I can decide for myself how wise he is." She ordered her servants to prepare a train of camels and load them with gifts for the king.

[2] After a few weeks, the queen was ready to set out. Throughout the long journey the queen rode her own camel. She sat on a silken cushion and was protected from the harsh sunlight by a silken canopy over her head. The journey across the desert was dangerous so many died from thirst or exhaustion. There were also fierce fights with bandits who wanted to steal the camels.

[3] When King Solomon knew that the queen was coming, he told his servants to polish the floor of his throne room floor until it was as shiny as a mirror and to set many lamps to blaze around the walls. The light from the torches reflected in the mirror-like floor so the room was bathed in dancing flames. King Solomon had heard a strange story about the queen. It was said that the beautiful queen had one leg that was hairy like a goat's and Solomon wanted to know if this was true.

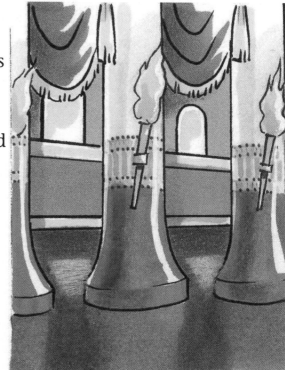

⁴ At long last, the queen's train of camels approached the palace. The king sent torch-bearers out into the desert to meet her so she came to his city in a glittering procession of torchlight. As he led the queen into his court, Solomon glanced down at the floor. It was true! She did have a hairy leg!

⁵ Soon the queen's leg was forgotten. King Solomon and the Queen of Sheba became good friends and the queen stayed at King Solomon's court for many months.

List three features that mean that this story is a legend:

1 _____

2 _____

3 _____

B Re-read the legend. Find these words in the text. Without looking at a dictionary, write what you think they mean.

1 tale _____

2 trader _____

3 advisers _____

4 train _____

5 silken _____

6 bathed _____

7 approached _____

Think about what the word means in the sentence it is part of.

5 Paragraphs

 A These words and phrases can be used to begin paragraphs. Sort them into three groups: *When? Where?* and *When and Where?* Write them in the diagram.

> Outside   ~~Yesterday~~   Eventually   In the year 2050   Under my bed
> Near the lake   During the night   Later   In the morning
> At six o'clock   In the garden   When she reached the castle

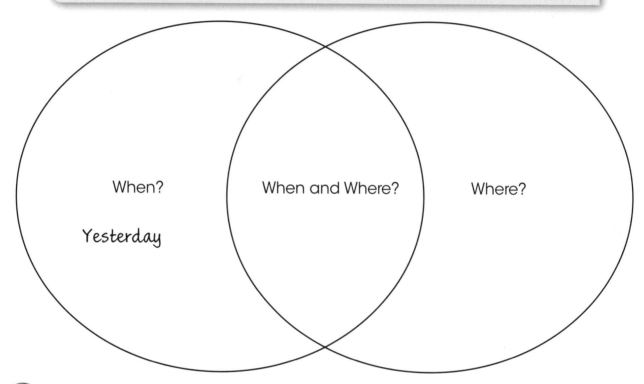

When?

Yesterday

When and Where?

Where?

B Complete the sentences with a suitable word or phrase from Activity A.

1 _____ the chief called a meeting and explained that the dragon was eating too many people.

2 _____ they decided to ask if anyone would fight the dragon.

3 _____ a girl said that she would like to try. Everyone laughed.

4 _____ the girl set off to find the dragon.

5 _____ she saw the dragon's cave.

6 _____ there was an enormous dragon.

6 Joining sentences

A Complete these definitions of simple and compound sentences.

1 A _____ sentence has only one verb or verb phrase. It

   starts with a _____ and ends

   with a _____ , question mark or

   exclamation mark.

2 A _____ sentence is made of two

   _____ sentences joined with the joining words

   _____ , _____ , *so* or *or*.

B Finish these sentences using your own ideas.

> Remember that you can use a pronoun instead of repeating a noun or noun phrase. You don't have to repeat the pronoun or noun if it is obvious who did the action.

1 The girl saw the enormous dragon and _____

   _____

2 The dragon yawned and _____

   _____

3 The dragon tried to make a flame but _____

   _____

4 The girl said, "Do you want to fight or _____

   _____ ?"

5 The dragon tried to fly away but _____

   _____ .

6 The girl lifted her spear so _____

   _____ .

7 The dragon burst into tears and _____

   _____ .

The monkey and the cat

A monkey and a cat once lived together with an old man. They were good friends.

One evening they were warming themselves by the fire. They could smell the delicious smell of the chestnuts that were roasting in the flames.

At last the monkey became so hungry that he tried to pick a chestnut out of the fire. "Ow!" he complained. "That's too hot! I can't get it!"

Then he looked slyly at the cat and said, "I have a plan. You are so much braver than me. A bit of pain won't worry you. If you put your paw into the fire and pull out the chestnuts, we can share them." The cat liked the monkey so she put her paw into the fire, just as her friend had asked her to do.

The cat began pulling the chestnuts out of the fire. But as fast as she pulled them out, the monkey grabbed them and gobbled them up.

After a while the old man picked up the cat and bandaged her burnt paw. "Poor old puss," he said. "I hope you have learnt a lesson from this."

A Read the fable then draw a picture to show the moral of the fable.

B Look at the **Language focus** box then write the past tense forms of the verbs.

Language focus

How to form the past tense of regular verbs

1. For most verbs, add *ed*: *Walk + ed → walked, pull + ed → pulled, pick + ed → picked.*

2. If the verb ends in *e*, add *d*: *live + d → lived.*

3. If the verb has one syllable with a short vowel followed by a single consonant, double the consonant and add *ed*: *grab → grabb + ed → grabbed.*

4. If the verb ends in *y*, change the *y* to an *i* and add *ed*: *try → tri + ed → tried.*

look → _____   cry → _____

carry → _____   lick → _____

smile → _____   ask → _____

reply → _____   notice → _____

like → _____   add → _____

8 More about fables

 A Match the beginning and ending of these sentences.

1. A myth   a   teaches a lesson or moral; the characters are often animals.

2. A legend   b   explains why or how something is as it is.

3. A fable   c   is about brave heroes or heroines who face dangerous tasks.

B Complete the table of pronouns.

Male	he	him	himself
Female	she		
Plural		them	
Neither male nor female			itself

9 Making links

A All these verbs can be used instead of *said* but they don't all mean the same!
Complete the table to show how they are different.

asked   demanded   murmured   screamed   sobbed

cried   enquired   muttered   shouted   wailed

declared   questioned   whispered

exclaimed   shrieked

How the words are said	Verbs
quietly	
in a questioning way	*asked*
loudly	
very loudly	
sadly	

Language focus

Punctuation marks are used to help the reader to make sense of the text.

. ! ?

Full stops, exclamation marks and question marks show the end of sentences.

, , ,

Commas separate items in lists and ideas in sentences.

' ' or " "

Speech marks show the beginning and end of speech

B Complete the text with the missing punctuation.

[ ] I have been listening to the traders," said the queen.

"What have you found out [ ]" asked her advisers [ ]

"They say that this new king is very wise, [ ] replied the queen.

"Have you heard the stories [ ] The man is already a legend [ ]

I want to find out how wise he really is. [ ]

10 Plan a fable

Working out the pattern of a known story lets you plan a new story based on the same pattern.

 A For this activity, first re-read 'Bear and Fire' on page 43. Then look at the table below. It shows a story pattern based on the stages of the 'Bear and Fire' story. Can you see how the pattern is made?

'Bear and Fire'	Pattern
Bear owned Fire.	introducing characters 1 and 2
Bear left Fire by the edge of the wood and wandered off. Fire got hungry	character 1 leaves character 2 character 2 needs character 1
Man came and fed Fire. Man and Fire became friends.	character 3 helps character 2 characters 2 and 3 become friends
Bear came back. Fire chased him away. Fire now belonged to Man.	character 1 returns character 2 chases character 1 away characters 2 and 3 stay friends

B Making a plan like the one in Activity A is called 'boxing up' a story. Try boxing up a different story based on the same pattern.

Pattern	New story
introducing characters 1 and 2	
character 1 leaves character 2 character 2 needs character 1	
character 3 helps character 2 characters 2 and 3 become friends	
character 1 returns character 2 chases character 1 away characters 2 and 3 stay friends	

11 Write a fable

A Copy the paragraph from the fable below.

How good is your handwriting?

Then he looked slyly at the cat and said, "I have a plan. You are so much braver than me. A bit of pain won't worry you. If you put your paw into the fire and pull out the chestnuts, we can share them." The cat liked the monkey so she put her paw into the fire, just as her friend had asked her to do. The cat began pulling the chestnuts out of the fire. But as fast as she pulled them out, the monkey grabbed them and gobbled them up.

_____

_____

_____

_____

_____

B Tick (✓) the statements that are true of your handwriting. Then write your own handwriting target.

- It is easy to read. ☐

- The tall letters and the letters that go below the line are a different size from the other letters. ☐

- All the other letters are the same size. ☐

- The spaces between the letters in a word are about the same size. ☐

- The spaces between the words are about the same size. ☐

- All of my writing is joined. ☐

- Some of my writing is joined. ☐

- None of my writing is joined. ☐

My handwriting target:

_____

A visit from strangers from another place

1   In the long ago past, there was a tribe of people who lived far, far away. They built their camp near a burning fire that never went out so that they could light their fire-sticks from it. They were the only people anywhere who had the use of fire.

2   One day, two brothers from the camp got bored and decided to go on a hunting trip to explore the world. "We will go and hunt possum," they agreed, "and bring back enough for everybody." So Kanbi and Jitabidi went out into the world and brought their fire-sticks with them. They left the sticks by a rock while they went hunting.

3   At first the fire-sticks were happy to lie and breathe in this strange new land. After a while, however, they became bored and started to play. They ran from place to place, and everywhere they ran the dry grass caught alight.

4   The fire grew and spread and roared and sent out black clouds of smoke. Kanbi and Jitabidi heard the flames and smelled the smoke and hurried back to put out the fire and collect their fire-sticks. However, the Aboriginal people who lived in that part of the world had also heard the flames and smelled the smoke. They came to see what was happening. They had never seen fire before so they were frightened of this loud, orange monster. As the fire came closer, they felt its heat and they bathed in its light.

5   Before Kanbi and Jitabidi could finish putting out the fires, some of the Aboriginal people had lit their own fire-sticks and were carrying them back to their camps. "We must watch over these fire-sticks carefully and keep them burning forever," they said to one another.

6   Kanbi and Jitabidi quickly gathered up their playful fire-sticks and returned to their campsite. They were afraid the Aboriginal people would punish them for the damage they had caused. But the people were excited and grateful for the wonderful gift of fire.

Read the Aboriginal story and answer the questions.

1   Is this story a myth, a legend or a fable? Explain your answer by giving two features of the genre that are in the story.

_____

_____

2   Read these statements about the strangers from another place. Tick (✓) two statements we know are true from the story.

   a   They lived far, far away.   ☐

   b   They lived on the sun.   ☐

   c   They had fire.   ☐

   d   They liked possums.   ☐

   e   They wanted to give fire to the rest of the world.   ☐

3   Why did Kanbi and Jitabidi come to where the Aboriginal people lived?

_____

4   How did Kanbi and Jitabidi know that there was a fire?

_____

5   What did the Aboriginal people think the fire was like?

_____

6   What made them like it better?

_____

7   In the last paragraph it says, 'They were afraid the Aboriginal people would punish them.' Who are 'they'?

_____

8   Which word in paragraph 2 is used instead of *said*?

_____

5 Letters

1 Letters and postcards

A What sort of mail comes to your house in a week? Complete the table each day (For example, letters, postcards, parcels, advertisements, newspapers.)

Day	What kind of mail?
Monday	
Tuesday	
Wednesday	
Thursday	
Friday	
Saturday	
Sunday	

B Draw a stamp from where you live.

C Design a stamp that you would like to be able to buy.

2 Scanning or reading carefully?

 Scan the text and answer the questions below.

Dear Mummy and Daddy,

We're having a good time with Grandmother.

We have just come back from a trip to the beach. It seemed to take a long time to get there and the beach was quite crowded. At first I thought that the trip was going to be a waste of time, but I soon changed my mind.

First Grandmother gave us money for a drink and we both felt better after that. Then she found an empty piece of beach and put up a sort of beach tent. It was great! We could change in private, and so we were soon splashing around in the water. When we came out, it was good to have the tent to get out of the sun. Can we get a tent like that?

I hope you are having a quiet time without us.

Lots of love,

Padma

1   Who is Padma staying with? _____

2   Where did they go? _____

3   What did they use the tent for? _____

B Read slowly and carefully to find the answers to these questions.

1   Is Padma staying with Grandmother by herself?

_____

2   How did Padma feel when she first got to the beach?

_____

3   Why did she get changed?

_____

3 A good day out

 A Draw lines to match words that can be synonyms.

big	tiny
little	terrible
good	pleasant
bad	massive
nice	pleased
nasty	miserable
silly	brilliant
odd	crazy
happy	strange
sad	horrid

Synonyms are words that have similar meanings.

 B Write sentences using the synonyms from Activity A.

Example: big _We saw a massive ship._

1 little _____

2 good _____

3 bad _____

4 nice _____

5 nasty _____

6 odd _____

7 happy _____

8 sad _____

9 silly _____

4 An interesting experience

 Choose one of the photos A–E. Imagine you were one of the people in the photo. Write notes about it.

Photo _____

What? _____

_____

Who? _____

When? _____

Where? _____

Why?/How? _____

Language focus

An apostrophe shows where two words have been joined together and then shortened: *you are → you're, they will → they'll.*

 Complete the tables to show the words in full and the shortened forms.

Words in full	Shortened form	Words in full	Shortened form
is not	isn't	I am	I'm
	can't		he's
would not		it is	
was not		we are	
	couldn't		they're
	aren't	I will	
were not			you'll
will not			we'll

5 Arturo's birthday

 Design your own party invitation. Remember to say

- why you're having a party
- the name of the guest
- the place, date and time of the party
- who the invitation is from.

Language focus

Remember the spelling rules for plural forms.

- For most words, just add s.
- If the word ends in *s, ss, sh, ch, x* or *zz*, add *es*.
- If the word ends in consonant + *y*, change the *y* to an *i* and add *es*.
- For some words that end in *f* or *fe*, change the *f* to a *v* and add *es*.
- For irregular plurals, there are different plural forms – you just have to know them.

B Write the plurals of these nouns.

You may need to use a dictionary or a thesaurus.

spoon _____   shoe _____

smile _____   glove _____

glass _____   half _____

knee _____   box _____

baby _____   wish _____

hen _____   moth _____

pencil _____   fly _____

monkey _____   wife _____

knife _____   donkey _____

man _____   mouse _____

6 A letter of complaint

A Join these pairs of sentences using *and, but, so* or *or.*

Example: Jake(likes)swimming. Jake(likes)playing cricket.

Jake likes swimming and he likes playing cricket. _____

1 Sanjay is good at football. He runs very fast.

_____

2 Sita remembered to wash her hands. She was ready for her meal.

_____

3 Paola is good at reading. Paola does not like writing.

_____

4 Would you like a drink? Would you prefer something to eat?

_____

B Read the letter to Arturo and circle all the pronouns in it.

> Remember that a pronoun is used instead of a noun or noun phrase (a group of words that act like a noun). The words *I, me, you, he, him, she, it, we, us, they* and *them* are all pronouns.

Dear Arturo,

I am enjoying the time we spend together. I like to go out with you and explore. I have lots of photos of us in London. We must show them to Mum and Dad so they can enjoy them too. I need to thank Mum for her camera. It has been very useful.

I know Dad likes to eat pizza. Shall we take him and Mum to that pizza restaurant we both like so he can eat as much of it as he likes?

Lots of love,

Aunty Sonia

C Complete the table with the pronouns that were used for each person or thing. You may need to write the same pronoun more than once.

Person or thing	Pronoun
Aunty Sonia	
Arturo	
Mum and Dad	
Dad	
photos	
camera	
pizza	

7 More about apostrophes

Dear Class 3,

[1] It's been a long time since I last wrote to you because my mother was in hospital for a few weeks. She had an operation last week and now she's getting better. That's good news, isn't it? I have now left my sister's house and I am staying with my mother at her house. I will stay with my mother until she is completely better.

[2] I was able to spend some time with Arturo last week. It was raining, so we had to stay inside. We spent an afternoon drawing pictures of things we have seen. I think Arturo's pictures were better than mine.

[3] When I know that my mother is really better, I'll book my ticket back to Argentina. I hope you're all behaving well and working hard.

From Mrs Sabella

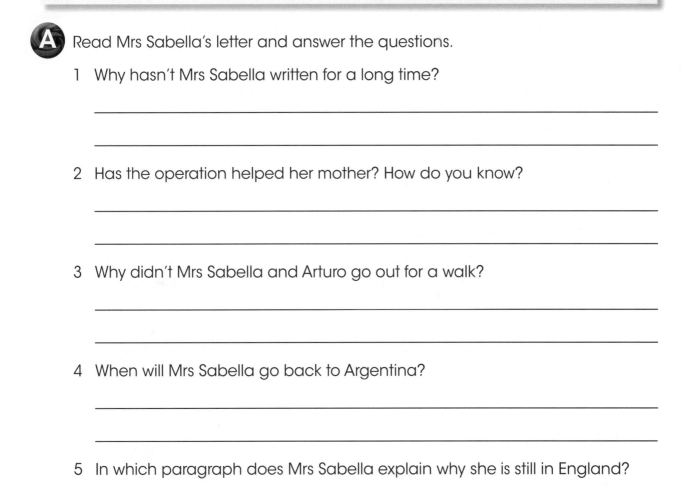

A Read Mrs Sabella's letter and answer the questions.

1 Why hasn't Mrs Sabella written for a long time?

_____

_____

2 Has the operation helped her mother? How do you know?

_____

_____

3 Why didn't Mrs Sabella and Arturo go out for a walk?

_____

_____

4 When will Mrs Sabella go back to Argentina?

_____

_____

5 In which paragraph does Mrs Sabella explain why she is still in England?

_____

B Complete these lists.

Examples: I will ___I'll___

1 they are _____

2 you would _____

   Mum has a camera

   ___Mum's camera___

3 Dad has a pizza

   _____

Examples: you'll ___you will___

4 couldn't _____

5 it's _____

6 won't _____

   Maja's house ___Maja has a house___
   ___/ the house of Maja___

7 Dani's pencil _____

> An apostrophe shows where two words have been joined together and then shortened. An apostrophe also shows possession.

8 Focus on writing

A Look at the first draft of Arturo's letter to his Aunty Sonia.

1 Cross out three common words and replace them with more powerful synonyms.

2 Make three compound sentences using joining words.

3 Correct three mistakes.

> Dear Aunty Sonia,
>
> Thank you for takeing me out today. I had a nice time. I liked it when we went on the big train. The train was big. It was shiny. It was green. I liked it when the train went through the tunnel. It made the smoke bloa in my hair.
>
> The cat is watching TV with me. Her kittens are playing. they are making a sound. It is a big sound. They are going around the room. The cat is purring.
>
> Lots of love,
>
> Arturo

> Did you remember that Arturo's Aunty Sonia is Mrs Sabella?

9 Going home

 Rewrite these messages using sentences with a verb or a verb phrase.

1   you at cricket yesterday? _____

2   I happy at your news. _____

3   They with Juanita at playtime. _____

4   You tea? _____

5   You good day at school? _____

 Read the letter and circle all the pronouns you can find. Then complete the table to show which pronouns are used instead of the nouns or noun phrases.

From: Sonia.Sabella@argentinamail.com

To: Arturo.Bilardo@email.co.uk

Subject: Missing you already

Dear Arturo,

I have been home for only three hours but they have been very busy! I had to collect my cats from Mrs Menotti. She looked after them while I was with you. She is very kind, but she wanted me to sit down and tell her all about you.

The plane I flew home in was very big. It had over 300 seats but they were very close together. Near me was a family. The three children didn't like sitting down for so long and kept running around. Looking at them made me think of you but I think you would have sat more quietly than they did.

I need to go to bed now. I have to go to school tomorrow and meet all the lovely children in Class 3. I wonder if they have missed me?

With very much love,

Aunty Sonia

Noun or noun phrase	Pronouns
Aunty Sonia	I, me
Arturo	
hours	
cats	
plane	
seats	
children on the plane	
children in Class 3	

10 All sorts of mail

A Read the two texts. Tick (✓) the statements that are true.

1 The letter is from Linda Matthews. ☐

2 The letter is from Mrs Evans. ☐

3 Linda is a friend of Mrs Evans. ☐

4 Linda is giving Mrs Evans information about her family. ☐

5 Linda wants Mrs Evans to go on holiday to Argentina. ☐

6 The purpose of the letter is to report news of events in Argentina. ☐

7 The purpose of the letter is to make Mrs Evans want to visit Argentina. ☐

8 The letter is fiction. ☐

9 The letter is non-fiction. ☐

Argentina Luxury Tour

An unforgettable experience

22-day holiday

All for just £1,195!!

Argentina holiday highlights:

- ❤ Visit Buenos Aires, city of culture.

- ❤ Go to a milonga and learn to dance the tango.

- ❤ Taste fantastic food.

- ❤ See the mighty Iguazu Falls.

- ❤ Explore the hot, humid Argentine rainforest.

Dear Mrs Evans,

Do you need a holiday?

Do you need a rest or are you looking for adventure?

Come to Argentina for your holiday of a lifetime!

Argentina is one of the world's largest countries. It is made for your perfect holiday!

Relax on a cruise off the Antarctic shores. Why not go whale-watching or swimming in the warm Southern Ocean?

Or have an adventure herding cattle as a gaucho in the Pampas grasslands!

If you like excitement, how about climbing in the Andes?

Or if cities are more your thing, just head for the vibrant city of Buenos Aires.

Other experiences not to be missed:

- Go to a football match at Boca Juniors or River Plate stadium.
- Drink a delicious cup of mate.
- Learn to tango.
- Swim in the South Atlantic from one of the beautiful beach resorts.

So what are you waiting for, Mrs Evans? Please come and join us in sunny Argentina!

Yours sincerely,

Linda Matthews
Customer Travel Advisor

 0044 1234 567890 *or*

 info@holidays_in_argentina.co.uk

B Find these sentences in the texts. What do the underlined words mean?

1 Go to a <u>milonga</u> and learn to dance the tango.

Milonga means _____ .

2 See the <u>mighty</u> Iguazu Falls.

Mighty means _____ .

3 Explore the hot, <u>humid</u> Argentine rainforest.

Humid means _____ .

4 Relax on a <u>cruise</u> off the Antarctic shores.

Cruise means _____ .

5 Have an adventure herding cattle as a <u>gaucho</u>.

Gaucho means _____ .

11 Writing a letter

 A Draw lines to join the everyday verbs on the left with the more interesting verbs on the right. Choose one matching verb for each one.

make	speak
like	stroll
do	glimpse
say	construct
walk	achieve
want	admire
see	desire

B Write the missing punctuation in this letter. Write any missing capital letters.

Dear Arturo

I cant believe that its been a week since I last saw you so much has happened in the week

I was so pleased to get back to school and meet Class 3 again I knew it would be exciting to hear about their lessons with the other teacher I asked them to write about what they had been doing since I last saw them they have been very busy

What have you been doing I wish I didnt live so far away it would be so good to see you more often

Love from Aunty Sonia

12 Improve your letter

A Complete the spelling log for five words you want to learn to spell.

Word	Tricky bit	Other words with the same spelling pattern		
learn	ear	earn	early	earth

1 Word pictures

Dancing Poinciana

Fire in the treetops,
Fire in the sky.
Blossoms red as sunset
Dazzling to the eye.

Dance, Poinciana,
Sway, Poinciana,
On a sea of green.
Dance, Poinciana,
Regal as a queen.

Fire in the treetops,
Fire in the sky.
Crimson petals and white
Stained with scarlet dye.

Dance, Poinciana,
Sway, Poinciana,
On a sea of green.
Dance, Poinciana,
Sway, Poinciana,
Regal as a queen.

Telcine Turner

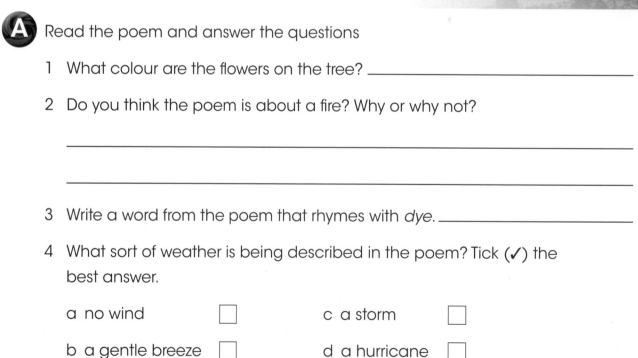

A Read the poem and answer the questions

1 What colour are the flowers on the tree? _____

2 Do you think the poem is about a fire? Why or why not?

_____

_____

3 Write a word from the poem that rhymes with *dye*. _____

4 What sort of weather is being described in the poem? Tick (✓) the best answer.

a no wind ☐

c a storm ☐

b a gentle breeze ☐

d a hurricane ☐

5 Explain your answer to question 5.

_____

_____

6 What does the word *regal* mean? Tick (✓) the best answer.

a real ☐   c funny ☐

b red   ☐   d noble ☐

2 Hurricane!

Language focus

For most verbs, just add *ing* to the end of the verb.
For verbs that end in *e*, take off the *e* and then add *ing*.
For verbs that have a short vowel followed by one consonant, double the consonant and then add *ing*.

Can you remember the rules for adding *ing* to verbs? Check you know what to do by looking at the Language focus box.

A Complete the lists of verbs and *ing* forms.

smile   → _smiling_   _____ → coming

say   → _____   dance   → _____

_____ → going   howl   → _____

run   → _____   _____ → staring

drop   → _____   fly   → _____

_____ → walking   _____ → pulling

like   → _____   _____ → flashing

_____ → standing   hurry   → _____

_____ → rushing   _____ → roaring

clap   → _____   become → _____

B Time yourself! In one minute how many *ing* forms of a verb can you find in this story? Underline all the ones you can find.

The king was counting his gold. "Bring me more gold!" he shouted.

His soldiers went running into the town. They saw children skipping and laughing, and the soldiers shouted to them, "Bring us your gold, your rings and your coins. The king needs more gold!"

Some people were standing nearby, looking at a pile of old clothes. They stopped looking and stood staring at the soldiers, not believing what they had just heard. Suddenly, everyone saw the pile of old clothes was standing up and it was talking.

"No!" said the pile of old clothes, which was really a very old man. "The king has been spending too much money too quickly. He must learn to save his money, not spend it."

So without giving the soldiers anything, the people went back into their houses, the parents carrying their children. And instead of running around, the soldiers walked slowly back to the palace to see the king. They told him what the very old man had said.

When they had finished telling their tale, the soldiers saw that the king was weeping. Tears were flowing down his cheeks, but he was smiling. "Bring the very old man to me," he said. "He is wise and I need his help."

3 More word pictures

The thunder is a great dragon

The thunder is a great dragon that lives in the water
and flies in the air.
He carries two stones.
When he strikes them together,
the lightning flashes and the thunder roars.
The dragon pursues the spirits of evil,
and wherever he finds them,
he slays them.
The evil spirits hide in the trees,
and the dragon destroys them.

A Read the poem and underline all of the words ending with the letter s. Decide whether the s shows a plural noun or a he/she/it form of a verb. Then complete the table.

Plural nouns with s	Verbs ending in s
stones	lives

Who remembers what simple and compound sentences are? Check in the Language focus box if you need reminding.

B Are the sentences simple sentences or compound sentences? Write S for simple and C for compound.

Language focus

A simple sentence has only one verb: *The dragon lives in the water.* Simple sentences can be joined together using joining words to make a compound sentence. A compound sentence is made up of two simple sentences joined with *and, but, so* or *or.* For example, *The dragon lives in the water and flies in the air.*

1 Thunder is a dragon. _____

2 The dragon can swim in the water or it can fly in the air.

_____

3 The dragon flies very high up in the sky but you can't see it.

_____

4 The dragon makes thunder and lightning. _____

5 The dragon strikes its stones together and starts a thunder storm.

_____

6 I saw a grey dragon and a black one. _____

Song of the animal world

Narrator: The fish goes
Chorus: Hip!
Narrator: The bird goes
Chorus: Viss!
Narrator: The monkey goes
Chorus: Gnan!

Fish: I start to the left,
I twist to the right.
I am the fish
That slips through the water,
That slides,
That twists,
That leaps!

Narrator: Everything lives,
Everything dances,
Everything sings.
Chorus: Hip! Viss! Gnan!

Bird: The bird flies away,
Flies, flies, flies,
Goes, returns, passes,
Climbs, floats, swoops.
I am the bird!

Narrator: Everything lives,
Everything dances,
Everything sings.
Chorus: Hip! Viss! Gnan!

Monkey: The monkey! From branch to branch
Runs, hops, jumps,
With his wife and baby,
Mouth stuffed full, tail in air,
Here's the monkey!
Here's the monkey!

Narrator: Everything lives,
Everything dances,
Everything sings.
Chorus: Hip! Viss! Gnan!

Read the poem and answer the questions.

1 Which creatures goes *Viss*?

_____

2 What do you think the word *viss* describes? Tick (✓) the best answer.

    a the sound the animal makes when it eats ☐

    b the sound the animal makes when it is angry ☐

    c the sound the animal makes when it moves ☐

    d the sound the animal makes when it sleeps ☐

3 Which way does the fish move first?

_____

4 Write another word from the poem that means the same as *slips.*

_____

5 Which word in the verse about the bird is the opposite of *goes*?

_____

6 Which word describes how the bird comes back down once it has flown

up high? _____

7 How does the monkey move?

_____

8 Who lives with the monkey?

_____

9 What do you think is in the monkey's mouth?

_____

10 Do you think this is a sad poem? Explain your answer.

_____

5 Moving like a cat

Suddenly awake.
Stretching, yawning, arching back,
stalking, pouncing: cat.

 Read the haiku about a cat. Then choose another animal for a haiku and complete the table about it.

Which animal?	
Five powerful **verbs** for what the animal does	
Five powerful **nouns** or **noun phrases** for what it looks like	
Something the creature does that other animals don't do	

 Use the words and phrases in your table to write a haiku about your chosen animal.

- A haiku has three lines:
- 5 syllables in line 1
- 7 syllables in line 2
- 5 syllables in line 3.

Remember that a haiku paints a very clear but very short picture of something.

Coral reef

I am a teeming city;
An underwater garden
Where fishes fly;
A lost forest
of skeleton trees;
A home for starry anemones;
A hiding place for frightened fishes;
A skulking place for prowling predators;
An alien world
Whose unseen monsters
Watch with luminous eyes.

Clare Bevan

 Read the extract from Clare Bevan's poem *Coral reef* and answer the questions.

1 Who is I in this poem?

_____

2 Who lives in this teeming city?

_____

3 List three different places that the coral reef is compared to.

_____

4 Do the fish really fly? Why do you think the poet used the verb fly?

_____

5 Which adjective is used to describe the anemones?

_____

7 Dragons and pirates

1 Adventures

A Which of these adventures would you most like to have? Choose one and write a short paragraph to explain why you would like to have this adventure.

_____

_____

_____

_____

_____

_____

B Add punctuation to this passage. Use full stops, capital letters, question marks, exclamation marks, commas and apostrophes.

fernando hurried after his brother and sister he didnt want to go but he knew they would never forgive him if he didnt he felt in the pockets of his shorts to see what he could find he found a piece of string three coins and his catapult he pulled out his catapult now he felt better he hurried on after his brother and sister

2 Story beginnings

 Tick the story beginnings that might be adventure stories.

1   The night was dark and the wind howled. Alone on the vast ocean a tiny boat bobbed up and down. Inside the boat, a small child lay sobbing. Suddenly, the child raised her head and screamed a single word: "Daddy!"

2   Tony the tiger walked to the flower shop.
"Hello," he said to Rupert the rhino. Rupert lived in the house next door to Tony's and owned the flower shop. Rupert was always happy in his shop.

3   "Why can't I be in the team?" sobbed Vincent. "I'm *nearly* eight. My birthday is in two months time."
"Don't cry, Vincent," said his mother. "It won't do you any good. Keep practising so that when you *are* eight you'll be good enough to join the team. Now come on, dry your eyes and let's go the market – we'll choose a nice fish for our dinner."

4   "Shhh!" whispered Petra. "You'll wake everyone up!"
Kaspar didn't say anything. He just hobbled after his sister's bobbing torchlight. His bag was heavy on his shoulder. He hadn't known how long they would be away so he had packed most of his belongings, just in case. They were going to find their uncle, but Kaspar wasn't sure why. Suddenly he felt frightened. He made a grab for his sister's hand but only got a handful of her dress. He kept tightly hold of it, feeling braver like that. Petra would keep him safe.

B Complete the following with adjectives from the box. For each one, decide whether you have made a noun phrase or a sentence. Write N for a noun phrase and S for a sentence.

> beautiful cracked deep everlasting fast frightened golden
> hidden long lost old ripe scary soft sweet tall twisted winding

1 the _____ snake _____

2 The tree is _____

3 The roots are _____ _____

4 a _____ branch

5 The sound was _____ _____

6 the _____ river

7 the _____ pool

8 The sand is _____ _____

9 some _____ fruit

10 The children are _____ _____

3 What happens next?

My name is Alfie Small, and I'm a famous explorer. I have lots of dangerous adventures and always take my rucksack with me, just in case!
At the bottom of my garden, behind the rickety shed, is the special place I go exploring.

The grass grows long and the weeds are tall and I never know what I might find.

Today, I pushed through the weeds … and found a small boat floating on a small stream.

So I climbed aboard and paddled away. The stream got bigger and the water flowed faster, and soon I was racing along as fast as a speedboat. I saw a huge boulder blocking the river. It was shaped like a dragon's head and my boat raced straight towards it. Help! I thought I was going to crash.

From *Dragons and Pirates* by Alfie Small

Read the text and answer the questions.

1 Read these statements. Tick (✓) two that you know are true from reading the text on the previous page.

a The person who is telling the story is a famous dentist. ☐

b Alfie Small takes his rucksack with him on his adventures. ☐

c Alfie lives near a river. ☐

d Alfie goes exploring in his shed. ☐

2 The shed is rickety. What does rickety mean? Tick (✓) the word that you think is closest in meaning.

a brown ☐

b small ☐

c old ☐

d wooden ☐

3 What did Alfie find behind the shed?

_____

4 Which words in the text tell you that the boat was going fast?

_____

5 What did the boulder remind Alfie of?

_____

B List all of the pronouns in the first paragraph.

4 Character portraits

 Who is Alfie Small? What is he like? What is he thinking and feeling when he is in the boat? Re-read the text from the previous session. Then choose at least six words from the box and use them in sentences to make a character portrait of Alfie, describing what he is like and what he does.

_____

_____

_____

_____

_____

_____

_____

_____

> curious   helpful   thoughtful   famous   lazy   interested   selfish   scared
> brave   boring   musical   imaginative   adventurous   unknown

5 Chapter headings

> Make **adjectives** using the suffixes *y* and *able*.
> Make **adverbs** using the suffix *ly*.
> Make **nouns** using the suffixes *ness* and *tion*.

 Look at the instructions in the box. Use the correct suffix to change the words.

Example: Make scare into an adjective. *scary*

1 Make slow into an adverb. _____

2 Make sad into a noun. _____

3 Make happy into an adverb. _____

4 Make sun into an adjective. _____

5 Make enjoy into a noun. _____

6 Make invite into a noun. _____

B Rewrite these simple sentences as complex sentences using *although, because, until* or *when.*

1 Alfie shouted for help. He was going to crash.

_____

_____

2 Alfie shut his eyes. He was swept into a tunnel.

_____

_____

3 He held on tight. The boat stopped spinning.

_____

_____

4 He kept on paddling. He didn't know where he was going.

_____

_____

_____

_____

6 A story about Alfie

A Look at these chapter headings from an adventure story. Which chapter do you think would be first? Which last? Write numbers 1–6 to show the order you think they would be in.

☐ A discovery on the beach

☐ Meet the Jacksons

☐ Home at last

☐ The holiday begins

☐ Danger!

☐ Escape

B Draw a picture of what you think the most exciting part of this story would be. Then write two sentences to explain what you have drawn.

_____

_____

"You see, Lily, the villagers needed fire to warm their homes, and cook their food, and make life good. So they chose the biggest, bravest man in the village. They gave him a fine spear and they called him Fire Snatcher. My da, your great-granda, Lily, was Fire Snatcher and hero of the village."

"But how did he snatch the fire?" asked Lily.

"Well, Lily, dragons are strange creatures," said Granda. "They lay their eggs, then sleep for a full ninety years until the eggs are ready to hatch. When that happens, the dragon mothers wake up to care for their babies. The dragons were in their sleep-years when my da was Fire Snatcher. All he had to do was creep, tiptoe-quiet into the hills, then jump, suddenly, on a sleeping dragon and poke it with his spear."

"The poor beast would start from its sleep and blaze with fright, just as you or I would if anybody jabbed at us with a needle while we were sleeping. But it worked. It made the dragon roar fire. As it roared, the Fire Snatcher thrust his torch of dry wood into the flare of the dragon's fiery breath to light it."

 Think about the Fire Snatcher as he goes to get the fire from the sleeping dragons. In each box write:

- three words to describe what you think the Fire Snatcher can see or hear

- three words to describe what he feels.

The Fire Snatcher leaves the village	He gets the fire	He returns to the village with the fire

8 Setting and dialogue

 What sort of setting do you think these adjectives belong to? Look at the three groups below and write the adjectives in the setting you think they would be useful for. Some may be useful in more than one setting.

> bright burning calm creepy dark gentle green
> gloomy glowing light mysterious quiet unhappy
> shadowy shining silent spiky spooky

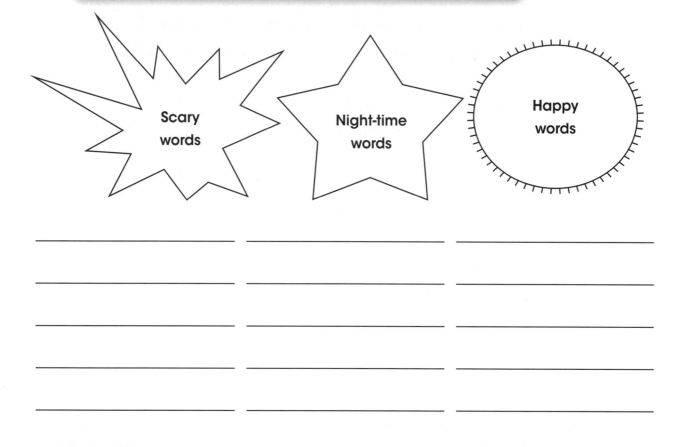

Scary words

Night-time words

Happy words

_____ _____ _____

_____ _____ _____

_____ _____ _____

_____ _____ _____

_____ _____ _____

_____ _____ _____

Language focus

Punctuate speech correctly.

- Use a new line for each speaker.
- Put ' or " at the beginning of the words that were said.
- Put ' or " at the end of them.
- Put question marks and exclamation marks before the closing speech mark.
- Don't forget the full stops.

B Look at this conversation about Dragon Boy. Add the missing punctuation in the small boxes. In each of the gaps write a word that could replace *said*. Choose from these words.

> answered asked demanded exclaimed interrupted
> laughed replied responded smiled wondered

☐Did Dragon Boy know that he was a human☐☐ _____

Lucy☐

☐No,☐ _____ Granda. "He grew up with dragons☐They

were his brothers and sisters and his friends☐☐

☐Could he do everything that they could do☐☐ _____

Lucy☐ Granda _____☐No, he couldn☐t fly. But most of

all he couldn☐t make fire☐That's what he wanted most☐☐

☐What happened to him☐☐ _____ Lucy☐

☐You☐ll have to wait and find out later,☐ _____

Granda☐

9 More about paragraphs

1   It was Cheng's first dragon hunt. He was scared but determined not to show it. Everyone had gathered in the village square. People held great wooden torches with flames dancing at the top. In the flickering light, Cheng looked for his sister.

2   At last Cheng found Huan. She was standing near the water pump with a group of her friends. She didn't look as scared as he felt, and that made him feel better. She caught his eye and winked at him but then turned back to her friends.

3   Suddenly Cheng heard the metallic boom of the gong. It was time to go. Cheng's mouth felt dry as he joined the back of the crowd. He was surrounded by the smell of burning wood, by the sound of hurrying feet. His eyes were watering from the smoke.

4   By the time they reached the mountains, Cheng was exhausted and lonely. He could just see Huan and her friends up ahead but he couldn't see his parents anywhere. None of his friends had wanted to come on the hunt. Cheng didn't blame them. He didn't want to be there either. He stopped and turned round.

5   Silently, he started walking back the way he had come. He listened to see if anyone called him, but no-one even noticed his departure. His eyes filled with tears.

6   Cheng turned a corner and there, in front of him, was a dragon.

A Read the beginning of an adventure story. Then complete the first part of the table to show the reasons the writer starts a new paragraph.

B Look again at the start of the paragraphs in the story. Do they begin with an adverb or adverbial phrase? If they do, write the word or phrase in the last part of the table.

Paragraph	Reason for new paragraph	Adverb or adverbial phrase?
1	start of story	–
2	different time	
3		
4	different time and place	
5		Silently
6		

Book review: *Dragon Boy* by Pippa Goodheart, illustrated by Martin Ursell

Dragon Boy is an engaging story about how it feels to be different – in this case, how it feels to be a human boy growing up amongst dragons.

At the start of the story, a young, nervous dragon accidentally sets fire to a village. The villagers run quickly away from the fire but they disturb the dragon's eggs. As the fire dies down, the young dragon goes to find her eggs and discovers that she has two babies – an ordinary dragon baby and a baby that is pink, soft and bald.

The young family grows up happily together: one baby grows into a beautiful green dragon and the other into a human boy. The boy loves his dragon family, but he feels different from them. However hard he tries he can't breathe fire like the other dragons. Eventually he learns more about himself and his human family.

The story is beautifully illustrated with colourful pictures and the book is an excellent read for children aged between 7 and 10. If you like myths and legends as well as stories about people, you will definitely enjoy finding out more about dragons and learning who Dragon Boy really is.

 Read the book review then answer these questions

1   Did the reviewer like the book? Write some words or phrases from the review to explain your answer.

_____

_____

2 Tick (✓) the items the writer has included in the review.

   a   the title of the book ☐

   b   the name of the person who wrote the book ☐

   c   the main events of the story ☐

   d   how the story ends ☐

   e   information about the main characters ☐

   f   reasons why people might want to read the book ☐

3 How old are the children who are most likely to enjoy the book?

_____

4 What other information about the book would you have liked there to have been in the review?

_____

B Read the book review then:

- Circle two adverbs or adverbial phrases that tell you *when* something happens.

- Circle two adverbs or adverbial phrases that tell you *how* something happens.

Adverbs or adverbial phrases are often placed at the beginning of a sentence. They can also be in the middle of a sentence, often near the verb. Many adverbs telling you how things happen end in *ly*.

11 Write a story

One day

In bed

The next day

After a week

Sadly

One day Gopal was bored. He went into his garden. He found an egg.
He picked it up. He took it home.
In bed later that night, Gopal looked at the egg. It was a big egg.
The next day the egg cracked. It was a dragon.
After a week the dragon made fire. It set the house
on fire.
Sadly, the dragon flew away.

 A Read the story. Do you think it is well written? Has the writer

- used any compound or complex sentences?

- given an interesting description of the characters?

- used any powerful or interesting words?

- included any dialogue?

*You could do better
than that!*

B Rewrite the story in your notebook. Remember to include:

- paragraphs

- character descriptions

- powerful and interesting words

- adverbs and adverbial phrases

- a mixture of simple, compound and complex sentences and a range of connectives

- dialogue.

12 Improve your story

 A Complete the list of past tense forms of these verbs.

buy → <u>bought</u>   find → _____

take → _____   fly → _____

catch → _____   throw → _____

say → _____   eat → _____

forget → _____   go → _____

B Choose five words from your writing that were difficult to spell. Write them in the first column of the spelling log and complete the log.

Word	Tricky bit	Word	Similar word

8 Wonderful world

1 Holidays

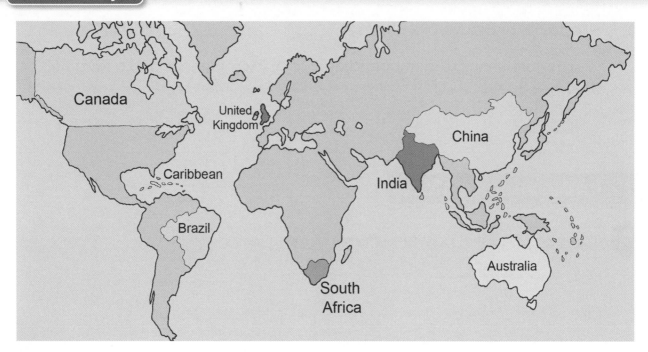

A Where in the world do you live? Draw a cross on the map to show the country you live in.

B Complete this text about where you live and where you like to go on holiday.

The name of the city I live in or near is _____ and the name of the country is _____ . People come here to see _____ and _____ .

When I go on holiday, I like to go to _____ because it has _____ and _____ . When I am on holiday I like to _____ and _____ .

Read these book titles. Do you think they are fiction or non-fiction? Write F or NF.

First Book of Sea Creatures

1 _____

Run, Dobbin, Run

2 _____

Escape from Mystery Mountain

3 _____

Top 10 Facts about Everything

4 _____

Learn to Draw

5 _____

The Magic Buttons

6 _____

Aliens from the Planet Glurgle

7 _____

Gardening for Beginners

8 _____

B Number these authors from 1 to 10 to show them in alphabetical order.

☐ June Crebbin   ☐ Michael Rosen

☐ Pippa Goodheart   ☐ Helen Cooper

☐ Thomas Docherty   ☐ Julia Jarman

☐ Adam Stower   ☐ Nick Sharratt

☐ Julia Donaldson   ☐ Allan Drummond

Look at this page from a book. Label the page with the features in the box.

text   glossary   heading   list   caption   diagram   subheading

Islands

1 _____

2 _____

An island is a piece of land that is completely surrounded by water. Some islands are very big. Others are small. Islands can be in cold places or in hot places. Some islands have large populations, others are **uninhabited***. Many islands were formed when volcanoes **erupted***. Examples of volcanic islands include the Canary islands, such as Tenerife and Lanzarote, and some of the Lesser Antilles islands in the Caribbean Sea.

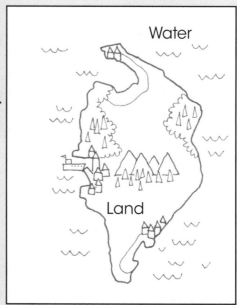
Water

Land

4 _____

Caribbean islands   3 _____

The Caribbean islands are a group of islands in the Caribbean Sea. They include the islands of

- Cuba
- Jamaica
- Barbados
- Antigua
- Saint Lucia.

5 _____

7 _____   6 _____   A beautiful beach on Antigua

uninhabited   *describes a place with no people living in it*

erupt   *when a volcano erupts, it explodes and flames and rocks come out of it*

Homes

Cities on Caribbean islands often have new and expensive flats in the centre. Cheaper houses are normally further out, around the edge of the city.

In Barbados, wooden houses built on stone blocks are called chattel houses. They can be moved to different places because they are not built into the ground. Chattel houses are often painted in pale colours to help keep them cool. The oldest chattel houses were built more than 200 years ago.

A Scan the text for the words in bold in these questions. Then answer the questions.

1 Which types of houses are in the **centre** of the cities?

_____

2 Why might some families live near the **edge of the city**?

_____

3 Which island has **chattel houses** on it?

_____

4 Why can chattel houses be **moved to different places**?

_____

5 How old are the **oldest chattel houses**?

_____

5 Using paragraphs

A These sentences come from a book about the Caribbean but they have got mixed up. Some belong in a paragraph about the sea, others belong in a paragraph about food. Read the sentences and write S if they are about the sea. Write F if they are about food.

1   The Caribbean Sea is a large sea. _____

2   People in the Caribbean grow a lot of the food they eat. _____

3   They have big gardens for their animals and food crops. _____

4   There are coral reefs in the sea around many of the Caribbean islands. _____

5   Colourful outdoor markets allow people to buy vegetables and spices they don't grow. _____

6   Colourful fish swim in and out of the corals. _____

7   People come to the Caribbean to dive in the clear, blue water. _____

8   There are many fish in the Caribbean Sea so people in the Caribbean eat a lot of fish. _____

B Complete the sentences with words from the box. Use each word once only.

> after   although   and   because   but   so   until

1   Some people visit the Caribbean for the holidays _____ other people live there.

2   Tourists enjoy sitting on the beach _____ swimming in the sea.

3   _____ it is called the dry season, it sometimes rains between December and May.

4   Hurricanes can be dangerous _____ of the strong winds.

5   People sit in storm shelters _____ the hurricane has passed away.

6   _____ the hurricane people have to clear up the island.

6 Language features of information texts

A Tick the sentences you might find in an information text about Uluru.

1   Have you been to Uluru? It's amazing! ☐

2   Uluru is one of Australia's best-known geographical features. ☐

3   First think about what you'll need to wear to climb up to the top. ☐

4   Uluru is near the Simpson Desert, where the sand is red. ☐

5   We watched the sun setting at Uluru, which was wonderful. ☐

6   Uluru was created about 600 million years ago. ☐

7   About 2.5 km of Uluru is underground. ☐

8   Visit Uluru! It's an unforgettable experience! ☐

B Write two more sentences about Uluru that could be part of an information text. Use the picture to help you.

_____

_____

_____

_____

7 Non-fiction e-texts

 A Complete the table of features of printed books and e-texts.

Books	e-texts	Purpose
contents page		tells you where you can find a topic
	heading	tells you what the topic is
main text		gives you information
index		helps you to find a particular word or idea
–		lets you move to other information linked to the topic
	photos and videos	illustrates information so you can see it as well as read about it

8 Plan a talk

 Think about the work you did on planning your talk. What did you do well and what could you have done better? Circle the mark out of 5 you would give yourself for how well you

- worked in your group

- researched your topic.

Working in a group

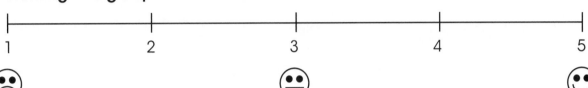

1   2   3   4   5

B Complete the notes about what you could do differently next time to make your work even better.

1   I did these things well:

_____

_____

2   I didn't do these things very well:

_____

_____

3   Next time I will do these things to make my work even better:

_____

_____

Researching my topic

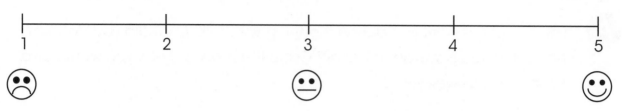

1 I did these things well:

_____

_____

2 I didn't do these things very well:

_____

_____

3 Next time I will do these things to make my work even better:

_____

_____

9 Give your talk

 Think about when you and your group gave your talk. What did you do well and what could you have done better? Circle the mark out of 5 you would give yourself for how well you

- presented your research

- listened to others.

B Complete the notes about what you could do differently next time to make your work even better.

Presenting my research

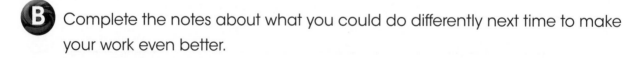

1 I did these things well:

_____

_____

2 I didn't do these things very well:

_____

_____

3 Next time I will do these things to make my work even better:

_____

_____

Listening to others

```
├────────┼────────┼────────┼────────┤
1        2        3        4        5
```

😞   😐   😊

1 I did these things well:

_____

_____

2 I didn't do these things very well:

_____

_____

3 Next time I will do these things to make my work even better:

_____

_____

Read this information text. Find and underline all the verbs. Has the writer used the present tense correctly? Correct the verbs that are in the wrong tense.

India

India is part of the continent of Asia. Most of the country was surrounded by water on three sides. The world's highest mountain range, the Himalayas, was rising in the north of India. The southeast is bordered by the Bay of Bengal, and the southwest was bordered by the Arabian Sea.

Geography of India

The land in India was very varied. The Thar desert in the west will be dry but the jungles in the northeast of the country were hot and wet. The Ganges Plain, which was covering most of northern India, is very fertile so it was a good place to grow crops.

Animals in India

There are nearly 2000 Bengal tigers in India and about 25 000 Indian elephants. Both these animals were now endangered animals. That is why many now lived in special protected areas called reserves. Indian culture respects

animals. Cows are holy animals and cannot be harmed. Cows wandered freely through the streets of big cities.

11 Write an information text

A Complete the lists of irregular verbs in the present and past tenses.

Present	Past		Present	Past
Examples: have	*had*		5 make	_____
go	went		6 _____	said
1 is	_____		7 write	_____
2 _____	were		8 _____	read
3 come	_____		9 find	_____
4 _____	did		10 _____	brought

B Complete these rules for adding *ed* to form the past tense of regular verbs.

1 For most verbs, add _____ .

2 If the verb ends in *e*, add _____ .

3 If the verb has one syllable with a short vowel followed by a single consonant (for example grin, clap), double the _____ , and add _____ .

4 If the verb ends in *y*, change the *y* to _____ and add _____ .

C Use the rules in Activity B to write the past tense of these regular verbs.

Present	Past		Present	Past
1 look	_____		6 hop	_____
2 like	_____		7 laugh	_____
3 lick	_____		8 try	_____
4 hunt	_____		9 skip	_____
5 carry	_____		10 hurry	_____

12 Improve your text

 Look again at the information text about India on page 106 and answer these questions.

1 Is India a continent? Explain your answer.

_____

2 Is India an island? Explain your answer.

_____

3 What is the mountain range in the North of India?

_____

4 Match the places on the left with the geographical descriptions on the right.

Himalayas	hot and wet
Thar desert	fertile
jungles	high
Ganges Plain	dry

5 Why do many Bengal tigers live in reserves?

_____

6 Why do cows wander on the roads in India?

_____

9 Laughing allowed

1 Jokes

Language focus

A **pun** is a play on words. Puns use a word that has several meanings or that sounds like another word. They work because you expect it to mean one thing but then it turns out to mean something else.

A Read these jokes. Which ones contain a pun? Tick (✓) the jokes that have puns in them and underline the words that have two meanings or that have been changed in some way.

1
What's a sea monster's favourite food?

Fish and ships!

2
What's worse than finding a caterpillar in your salad?

Yuck! I don't know. What's worse than finding a caterpillar in your salad?

Finding half a caterpillar in your salad!

7
What has four legs but can't walk?

Two pairs of trousers!

4
Tell me, Captain, how far are we from land?

About two miles, sir.

In which direction?

Downwards!

Where would you find a prehistoric cow?

In a mooseum!

3

Waiter, waiter – I'm in a hurry. Will my pizza be long?

No, madam. It'll be round like everyone else's.

6

5
Waiter, waiter – what kind of soup is this?

It's bean soup, sir.

I don't care what it's been – what is it now?

B Write two sentences for each of these words to show the different meanings they can have.

1 bank

_____

_____

2 can

_____

_____

3 kind

_____

_____

4 rock

_____

_____

5 row

_____

_____

6 trip

_____

_____

Good morning, Mr Croco-doco-dile

Good morning, Mr Croco-doco-dile,
And how are you today?
I like to see you croco-smoco-smile
In your croco-woco-way.

From the tip of your beautiful croco-toco-tail
To your croco-hoco-head
You seem to me so croco-stoco-still
As if you're coco-doco-dead.

Perhaps if I touch your croco-cloco-claw
Or your croco-snoco-snout,
Or get up close to your croco-joco-jaw
I shall very soon find out.

But suddenly I croco-soco-see
In your croco-oco-eye
A curious kind of croco-gloco-gleam,
So I just don't think I'll try.

Forgive me, Mr Croco-doco-dile
But it's time I was away.
Let's talk a little croco-woco-while
Another croco-doco-day.

Charles Causley

A Read the poem and answer the questions.

1 Number the events to show the order in which the speaker does them in the poem:

[ ] He sees a gleam in the crocodile's eye.

[ ] He thinks the crocodile looks as if it's dead.

[ ] He decides not to touch the crocodile's snout.

[ ] He plans to touch the crocodile's snout.

2 What is the last thing that the speaker does in the poem?

_____

3 Look at the first verse again. Tick (✓) all the sentences which explain how the poet plays with the *crocodile's* name.

[ ] He puts some silly sounds in the word *crocodile*.

[ ] He splits the word crocodile into three parts.

[ ] The first part is always *croco*.

[ ] Each part has two syllables.

[ ] All three parts rhyme with each other.

[ ] The first and second parts rhyme with each other.

[ ] The second and third parts always begin with the same sound.

B Scan these words. Circle all the irregular past tense forms you can find.

were	night	cat	ate	out	bought	laughed
round	was	said	third	thud	thought	tent
went	sight	is	found	sheep	sank	did	taped
board	packet	packed	cried	forgot	put

3 Funny poems and limericks

 A Help! Some of the words from this poem have got lost. Complete the poem with the word from the brackets you think best fits each gap.

The alien

The alien
Was as round as the moon.
Five legs he had
And his ears played a [1] _____ . (June/room/spoon/tune)
His hair was pink
And his knees were green,
He was the funniest thing I'd [2] _____ . (been/seen/mean/dream)
As he danced in the door
Of his strange [3] _____ , (car/spaceship/spacecraft/planet)
He looked at me –
And laughed and laughed.

Julie Holder

B What do you imagine the alien looks like? Use the information in the poem to draw the alien.

4 Calligrams and mnemonics

A Look at the calligrams. Then draw calligrams for three of these words.

fast   slow   under   squashy

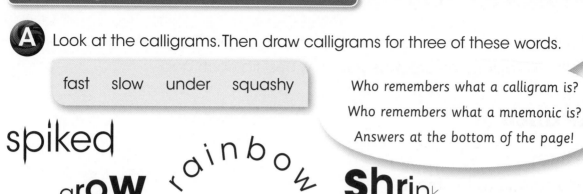

spiked   grOW   rainbow   Shrink

Who remembers what a calligram is?

Who remembers what a mnemonic is?

Answers at the bottom of the page!

B Choose a word you find hard to spell. Write a mnemonic to remind you how to spell it. Draw a picture to help you to remember it.

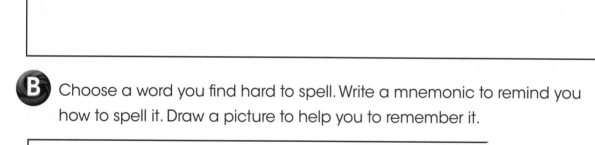

If you can't think of a word, how about *any, both, have, every, give, many* or *often*?

Answers: A calligram is the name of a poem or word that looks like its meaning.
A mnemonic is a saying that helps to remind you of a spelling or meaning.

5 Write a poem

Peter Piper picked a peck of pickled peppers.
A peck of pickled peppers Peter Piper picked.
If Peter Piper picked a peck of pickled peppers,
Where's the peck of pickled peppers that Peter Piper picked?

She sells seashells on the seashore.
The shells she sells are seashells, I'm sure.
For if she sells seashells on the seashore,
Then I'm sure she sells seashore shells.

A Read these tongue-twisters. Can you say them out loud – without making any mistakes? Play a game to see who can say them the fastest!

B Try writing your own tongue-twister. It doesn't have to be a poem. You could use some of these words in your tongue-twister.

rabbit   rain   race   read   rhino   ring   roll

walk   watch   wave   weigh   whale   warm   worm

_____

_____

_____

_____

_____

_____

_____

There was an old man of Dumbree,
Who taught little owls to drink tea;
For he said "To eat mice
Is not proper or nice,"
That amiable man of Dumbree.

Edward Lear

A Read the limerick. Clap out the rhythm. Now finish this limerick with your own ideas. Try and make your words fit the rhythm and rhyme pattern of a limerick.

There was ————————————————— from Niger,

Who ————————————————— with a tiger;

They went ————————————————— .

And ————————————————— ,

That ————————————————— from Niger.

B Look at all the different sorts of texts you have read in Unit 9. Which did you find funny? Which were clever? And which did you think were memorable? Perhaps you thought some of them were funny and clever, or clever and memorable … and perhaps some of them were all three! Complete the diagram on page 117, writing the different sorts of texts in the best section of the diagram for you.

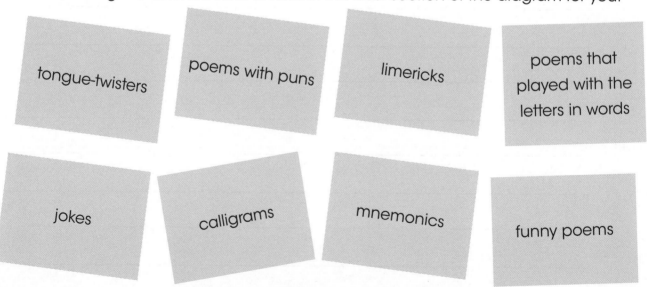

tongue-twisters

poems with puns

limericks

poems that played with the letters in words

jokes

calligrams

mnemonics

funny poems

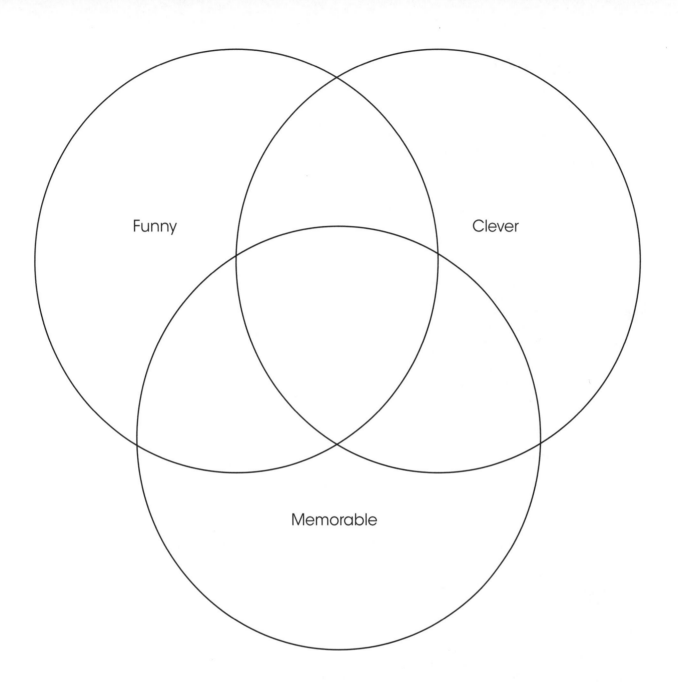

Funny

Clever

Memorable

Acknowledgements

The authors and publishers acknowledge the following sources of copyright material and are grateful for the permissions granted. While every effort has been made, it has not always been possible to identify the sources of all the material used, or to trace all copyright holders. If any omissions are brought to our notice, we will be happy to include the appropriate acknowledgements on reprinting.

Text

p. 5 *Once Upon an Ordinary School Day* by Colin McNaughton, published by Andersen Press, 2004; p. 15 excerpt from *Amazing Grace* by Mary Hoffman, published by Frances Lincoln, 1991; p. 43 'Bear and fire' used with permission from S.E. Schlosser and AmericanFolklore.net. Copyright 2014. All rights reserved; p. 72 'Dancing Poinciana' by Telcine Turner, used with permission; p. 79 Lines from 'Coral Reef' by Clare Bevan, used with permission of the author; pp. 82, 84 text and illustrations from *Alfie Small Pirates and Dragons* and *Alfie Small Ug and the Dinosaurs* by Nick Ward, published by Random House Children's Publishers, used by permission of The Random House Group; pp. 84 text and illustrations from *Dragon Boy* by Pippa Goodhart, illustrated by Martin Ursell, published by Egmont UK Ltd and used with permission, text © 2003 Pippa Goodhart, illustrations © 2003 Martin Ursell; p. 111 'Mr Croco-doco-dile' by Carles Causley, from *I had a Little Cat - Collected Poems for Children* (Macmillan), by permission of David Higham Associates; p. 113 'The Alien' by Julie Holder, first published by Oxford University Press, used by permission of the author

Cover artwork: Bill Bolton

The publisher is grateful to the following expert reviewers: Nahid Ali, Annick Cooper, Lois Hopkins, Mary Millet, Iram Mohsin.

Photographs

21 © Richard Hobson / iStock.com / Thinkstock; p33 *t l-r* © Noam Armonn / Hemera / Thinkstock, © Fuse / Thinkstock, © Sarah_Cheriton / iStock / Thinkstock; *b l-r* © Fuse / Thinkstock, © aseppa / iStock / Thinkstock; p40 © Bullyphoto / iStock.com / Thinkstock; p61 *A* © monkeybusinessimages / iStock.com / Thinkstock; *B* © onfilm / iStock; *C* © Fuse / Thinkstock; *D* © Fuse / Thinkstock; *E* © Digital Vision / Photodisc / Thinkstock; p64 © Purestock / Thinkstock; p69 *t* © javarman3 / iStock.com / Thinkstock; b © vau902 / iStock.com / Thinkstock; p72 © Jack Hollingsworth / Photodisc / Thinkstock; p78 © Wavetop / iStock.com / Thinkstock; p79 © mychadre77 / iStock.com / Thinkstock; p80 *l-r* © Darrin Klimek / Photodisc / Thinkstock, © Purestock / Thinkstock, © Wojciech Gajda / iStock.com / Thinkstock, © Frozentime Images / iStock.com / Thinkstock; p98 © Henrik Winther / iStock.com / Thinkstock; p101 © elcamilo / Thinkstock; p106 © narokzaad / iStock Editorial / Thinkstock; p108 © cenk unver / iStock Editorial / Thinkstock

Key: t = top, c = centre, b = bottom, l = left, r = right.